VIETNAM
the land

Bobbie Kalman

A Bobbie Kalman Book

The Lands, Peoples, and Cultures Series

Crabtree Publishing Company

www.crabtreebooks.com

The Lands, Peoples, and Cultures Series

Created by Bobbie Kalman

For Marc Crabtree,
my son—the awesome photographer

Written by
Bobbie Kalman

Coordinating editor
Ellen Rodger

Editor
Jane Lewis

Contributing editors
Kate Calder
P.A. Finlay
Carrie Gleason

Editors/first edition
Greg Nickles
Virginia Mainprize
Niki Walker
Dave Schimpky

Production coordinator
Rose Gowsell

Design and production
Text Etc.

Separations and film
Quadratone Graphics Ltd.

Printer
Worzalla Publishing Company

Consultant
Nancy Tingley, Wattis Curator of Southeast Asian
Art, Asian Art Museum of San Francisco

Special thanks to
Marc Crabtree, who, during a recent assignment in
Vietnam, took photographs that gave an accurate
portrayal of modern Vietnam; Lance Woodruff; Pierre
Vachon and the Canadian International Development
Agency; the Vietnam Canada Trade Council; the
World Society for the Protection of Animals

Photographs
Dave Bartruff/Corbis/Magmaphoto: p. 16, 17 (left);
Jeanette Andrews-Bertheau: p. 22 (bottom), 23 (bottom),
24 (bottom); Samantha Brown: p. 3, 4-5, 10 (bottom
right), 19, 21 (bottom), 22 (top), 29 (bottom);
CIDA Photo/Cindy Andrew: p. 13 (bottom); Marc
Crabtree: p. 1, 7, 8 (top), 10-11, 12, 18, 20, 21 (top), 23
(top), 24 (top), 25 (top), 27, 29 (top & middle); Hulton
Archive/Getty Images: p. 13 (top), 15 (both); Wolfgang
Kaehler: cover, p. 6, 8 (bottom), 9 (top), 10 (bottom left),
17 (right), 24 (middle), 26; Stuart McDonald: p. 25
(bottom); Tim Page/Corbis/Magmaphoto: p. 14 (top);
Rebmann/Explorer/Photo Researchers: p. 9 (bottom);
Steve Raymer/Corbis/Magmaphoto: p. 31 (bottom);
Larry Tackett/Tom Stack & Associates: p. 28; Nik
Wheeler/Corbis/Magmaphoto: p. 14 (bottom)

Every effort has been made to obtain the appropriate credit
and full copyright clearance for all images in this book. Any
oversights, despite Crabtree's greatest precautions, will be
corrected in future editions.

Illustrations
Scott Mooney : icons
David Wysotski, Allure Illustrations: back cover

Cover: Everyday, people from the fishing village of
Wha Trang, on Vietnam's eastern coast, head out to
the sea to fish.

Title page: Crops are grown on terraces that wrap
around mountainsides.

Icon: A dragon wing sailboat.

Back cover: Water buffalo are used in farming.

Published by
Crabtree Publishing Company

PMB 16A,	612 Welland Avenue	73 Lime Walk
350 Fifth Avenue	St. Catharines	Headington
Suite 3308	Ontario, Canada	Oxford OX3 7AD
New York	L2M 5V6	United Kingdom
N.Y. 10118		

Cataloging in Publication Data
Kalman, Bobbie, 1947-
    Vietnam. The land / Bobbie Kalman.-- Rev. ed.
        p. cm. -- (The Lands, peoples, and cultures series)
    Includes index.
    Summary: Describes the geography, climate, history, cities,
agriculture, transportation, business and trade, and wildlife of
Vietnam.
        ISBN 0-7787-9355-9 (RLB) -- ISBN 0-7787-9723-6 (pbk.)
        1. Vietnam--Juvenile literature. [1. Vietnam.] I. Title. II.
Series.
    DS556.3 .K36 2002
    959.7--dc21
                                                2001047107
                                                LC

Contents

A diverse land

Vietnam is a land of natural beauty with magnificent mountains, lush rainforests, fertile farmlands, and spectacular beaches. When many people think of Vietnam, however, they remember a country that was devastated by a terrible war in the 1960s and 1970s and caught up in border attacks during the 1980s. This fighting in Vietnam was only a short part of the country's long, eventful history.

A peaceful nation

Today, Vietnam is a peaceful and growing nation. Cities such as Ho Chi Minh City and Hanoi have developed into busy, modern urban centers. Traditional Vietnamese culture still thrives in many places, especially rural areas. Vietnam overcame many difficulties in the last century, and is now an interesting mix of history, tradition, and modern growth.

Facts at a glance

Official name: Socialist Republic of Vietnam

Capital City: Hanoi

Population: 78,773,873

Area: 125,708 square miles

(325,560 square kilometers)

Official language: Vietnamese

Main religion: Buddhism

Currency: New dong

North to south

Vietnam is a long, narrow country located in Southeast Asia. From north to south, Vietnam is nearly 1,000 miles (1,600 kilometers) long. It is bordered by China to the north and Laos and Cambodia to the west. The South China Sea lies to the east and south. The Vietnamese say their country is shaped like a bent bamboo pole carrying a rice basket at each end. If you look at the map, you will see that Vietnam has an S-shape. It is wide at the top and bottom and narrow at the center. The country is divided into three geographic regions, the north, center, and south.

Mountains and hills

Throughout northern and central Vietnam are hills and mountainous regions called the highlands. Thick forests of valuable hardwood trees cover half the highlands. The jungles are home to wild animals such as tigers and elephants. A quarter of Vietnam's population lives in villages throughout the highlands.

The Truong Son mountain range runs from the north into the south and separates Vietnam from Laos and Cambodia, its neighbors to the west. The Hoang Lien mountain range rises in the north, crossing from northern Vietnam into southern China. These mountains are higher and rockier than those of the Truong Son and include Vietnam's highest peak, Fan Si Pan.

The northern highlands

The northern region of Vietnam, called Bac Do, has two very different landscapes—the rugged highlands and the flat lowlands. In the highlands, some areas are still covered by dense jungle forests, but in others, the trees have been cut down for lumber or to clear land for farms. This area, rich in coal, tin, zinc, and lead, is also mined for these valuable minerals. Farmers and their families live in small villages scattered throughout the mountains and hills. They grow crops by building **terraces** on the rough hillsides.

(below) The hilly regions of northern Vietnam.

6

So much water!

More than two hundred rivers flow down from the mountains to Vietnam's long sea coast. The lowlands, between the mountains and the coast, are crisscrossed by rivers. The two longest, the Red River in the north and the Mekong River in the south, have formed wide, flat deltas. Most of Vietnam's population lives in lowland areas, either on farms or in large, busy cities.

The Red River and its delta

The Red River flows from China, down through the northern highlands on its way to the sea. Its water, reddish in color because of the silt it carries, has given the river its name. The wet, flat lowland area in Bac Do is the Red River Delta, home to millions of Vietnamese. Hanoi, the country's capital city, and Haiphong, a major seaport, are also in this delta.

Floods

In the lowlands, the Red River floods its banks each year during the rainy season. The floods, which dump silt onto the fields, are important to millions of farmers. In this rich, wet earth they grow rice. Throughout the delta, canals have been dug, and walls of earth, called dikes and levees, have been built to help control the water flow and divert it to the rice fields.

River deltas

The place where a river begins is called its source. As a river flows from its source, it picks up silt, or particles of soil and sand. The fast-moving water carries these particles along. When the river reaches the sea, the current slows suddenly. The soil and sand sink and begin to pile up.

Over hundreds of years, the pile grows and blocks the mouth of the river. The river splits into two branches and flows around the pile. Over time, each branch becomes clogged, and the water must find new paths. Eventually, a network of streams and channels forms around the river's mouth. This network is called a river delta. Delta soil, known as silt, is very good for farming. It is rich in the nutrients that plants need. This wet, marshy land is also home to a wide variety of birds, reptiles, mammals, and aquatic life.

(below) Floods create the right conditions for growing rice in Vietnam. Rice is the country's most important crop and source of food.

The central highlands

The central region, called Trung Bo, is the narrowest part of Vietnam. The Truong Son Mountains form the hilly central highlands, where tea plants and rubber trees are grown. Hill people, named *Montagnards,* "highlanders", by the French, live in the central highlands. Although there are several tribes, the population in this area is sparse. Farming is poorer here than in the fertile lowland deltas.

The coast

Most people in Trung Bo live along the long, narrow coast. They live in seaports, fishing villages, and on farms. Each day, thousands of boats head out to gather their catch of fish, a favorite food of many Vietnamese. Tourists enjoy visiting the scenic beaches along the South China Sea. This coast is beginning to change as new restaurants, hotels, and holiday resorts are being built.

(above) The hills rise behind this small village in the central highlands. Small areas of rainforest still exist in this part of the country.

(above) This beach along the central coast near Nha Trang is an excellent spot for water sports such as fishing, snorkeling, and scuba diving.

Southern lowlands

Nam Bo is Vietnam's southern region. It is a large, wet lowland area that contains the Mekong River Delta and several smaller deltas. Ho Chi Minh City is near the Mekong Delta. It is Vietnam's largest city and home to millions of people. Millions more live nearby in the fertile farmlands of the delta—one of the richest farming regions in the world. Canals cross this low, wet area, carrying water to the rice crops and transporting people and their goods.

Nine Dragons

The Vietnamese call the Mekong River "Nine Dragons" because it once had nine branches which flowed through Vietnam. The Mekong River is Asia's longest river. Starting in the mountains of Tibet, it runs through China, Laos, and Cambodia before branching several times at the Mekong Delta. It empties into the South China Sea.

(above) The Mekong River provides an easy way to transport goods to market.

(above) Thousands of families make their homes on boats near cities along the Mekong River. The river is more than 2,600 miles (4,186 kilometers) long.

Climate

Vietnam is a tropical country. Tropical areas lie between the Tropic of Cancer and the Tropic of Capricorn, two horizontal lines near the **equator**. Tropical countries have warm weather most of the year. Vietnam is such a long country that the weather in the north and south can be quite different. **Altitude** also influences climate. Weather in the highlands, which has a higher altitude, is cooler than in the lowlands. In the northern highlands, winter weather can become cool and frosty. Southern Vietnam is closer to the equator, so it is hot and humid all year long.

The monsoon

Vietnam's weather is affected by winds called **monsoons**. From October to March, the monsoons blow from the northeast, overland from China, bringing dry weather. From May to September, the monsoons come from the opposite direction, sweeping up from the southwest. They blow across the ocean, picking up water and forming rain clouds. When these monsoons hit land, the clouds dump heavy rains, which can cause severe flooding.

Water everywhere

Dikes and levees usually control the floods, but sometimes water rushes over them and causes terrible damage. Houses near the water are built on stilts so the flood waters can flow underneath. Even on stilts, homes can be damaged and sometimes people and animals drown. Despite the damage monsoon rains can cause, farmers depend on the rains and floods to bring water to their crops and fertile soil to their farmland.

Typhoon!

During the summer, violent tropical storms called typhoons form over the Pacific Ocean and batter the coast. Typhoons bring thunderstorms, crashing waves, high winds, and heavy rains. Weather forecasters are able to give warnings when these storms are approaching, but people can do little to prevent the damage they cause.

(above) During the summer monsoon, heavy rains fall on Vietnam. Umbrellas are a common sight on the streets during that time!

(opposite page, left) Hats and plastic raincoats are little protection against the monsoon rains.

(opposite page, right) Flood levels are recorded each year on the stilts that support this house. Flood levels in the year 2000 were dangerously high.

Vietnam's past

Vietnam's earliest history is told in legends. Some historians believe that the Vietnamese people's roots can be traced back to the ancient Viet, or Yue, people from China. Others believe that the ancient civilizations that lived in the area before the Viets have Malaysian characteristics. Over the centuries, a mixture of ancient Vietnamese civilizations spread into the highlands and coasts. By 2 A.D., the Viet kingdom of Nam Viet ruled the northern region.

Chinese rule

The Chinese invaded Nam Viet in 111 B.C. and controlled the region for over 1000 years. The Viet people had developed a distinct culture from China, and did not like their Chinese rulers. The Chinese introduced their forms of writing, farming, science, and government.

The Viets tried to overthrow their Chinese rulers many times. One famous revolt was led by two women, the Trung sisters, in 39 A.D. Trung Trac and Trung Nhi ruled the country for three years before the Chinese took over again. The two sisters refused to surrender to the Chinese, and threw themselves in the Hau Giang River.

Independence

In 938 A.D., the Viets finally defeated the Chinese army. For most of the next 900 years, the country was independent, ruled by several dynasties, or families. At the head of each dynasty was an emperor. One notable early dynasty was the Ly Dynasty. They called the country Dai Viet. The Ly emperors ruled from 1010 to 1225. They encouraged much political, economic, and cultural development.

(above) This temple was once part of Champa, a powerful kingdom in central Vietnam. The Cham people were strongly influenced by traders from India. Champa architecture is similar to the ancient Hindu architecture of India.

Expanding the nation

Each Vietnamese dynasty took over more land and expanded the Viet nation to the south. Two kingdoms that were conquered by the Viet people were the Champa kingdom of central Vietnam and the Khmer empire in the Mekong Delta of the far south. In 1802, under the Nguyen Dynasty, the country became known by its present name—Vietnam.

The colonial years

In the 1500s, Europeans from France, Spain, and Britain sailed to Southeast Asia to buy products such as rice, silk, tea, and spices. The French saw that Vietnam had rich, fertile farmland, **natural resources**, and mineral deposits that could be used to make money for France. French soldiers were sent to take over Vietnam and, by the late 1800s, France had claimed the country as its colony. A colony is a land controlled by a distant ruler.

French rule

The period of French colonial rule was devastating for Vietnam. The French government developed large rubber and tea **plantations**, built factories, and dug mines. They forced the Vietnamese people to work on the plantations. They built **Christian** churches and tried to change the religion of the Vietnamese. Vietnamese people had to pay high taxes and were not allowed to hold any important positions in government or business. Farmers revolted against their cruel landlords, and workers organized strikes, but the French stayed in control until World War II. During World War II, Japan took control of Vietnam for five years. After the war and the Japanese surrender in 1945, the Vietnamese hoped to form an independent country with their own leaders. France, however, wanted its colonies back. Soldiers were sent and, within a few months, France again controlled Vietnam.

(above) Nguyen Vinh Thuy, known by the title "Bao Dai," was the last emperor to reign in Vietnam. He was twelve years old when he became emperor in 1925.

(right) The French built many churches and converted people to Christianity.

13

War

The Vietnamese were determined to end French rule. One of the Vietnamese leaders who fought to end French rule was a man named Ho Chi Minh. He was the leader of the **Communist** Party in Vietnam. After eight years of fighting against the French, Northern Vietnam gained independence. With Ho Chi Minh as its leader, North Vietnam sought to control South Vietnam. The south was led by a **corrupt** government, supported by France and the United States.

A bloody fight

The North Vietnamese army and the **Viet Cong** began attacking villages in the south. In 1964, the United States sent in thousands of soldiers to help South Vietnam. They called this fight the Vietnam War. This terrible, bloody war lasted for more than eleven years. Soldiers fought in fields, swamps, jungles, and villages. The Americans killed people they thought were on the side of the Viet Cong; the Viet Cong killed people they thought were helping the Americans.

A nation lost

Thousands of bombs were dropped on the north and south. About two million Vietnamese were killed, four million were injured, and six million lost their homes. By 1973, when the United States withdrew its troops, 58,000 American soldiers were dead or missing.

Agent Orange

During the war, the Viet Cong often hid in the thick jungles of South Vietnam. American planes dropped a chemical called Agent Orange onto the jungles to kill the trees, which would uncover the hideouts of the enemy soldiers. Agent Orange was very destructive, killing trees, poisoning the water and soil, and destroying crops. Many people starved to death. People and animals were sometimes sprayed by passing planes. Since the war, the chemical has been blamed for causing disease and birth defects.

(top) For more than eleven years, soldiers from North and South Vietnam fought one another.

(below) The Vietnam War caused a tremendous amount of destruction across the country.

Running from the war

The people of Vietnam suffered greatly during the war. Their villages were burned, cities were bombed, farms were destroyed, and innocent people were killed. Thousands of people were forced to live in **refugee** camps outside the cities because they had no homes, jobs, or money. After the war, a million people left Vietnam, seeking a safer place to live. Thousands died at sea while trying to escape in overcrowded boats. People who escaped by boat were known as the "boat people."

The battles continue

The end of the war with America did not bring peace. Vietnam and Cambodia had been disputing border areas since before the war. Political differences with Cambodia, which was in the midst of its own revolution, lead to fighting between the two countries. In support of Cambodia, China attacked Vietnam for 17 days in 1979. Millions of Cambodian and Vietnamese people suffered and were killed during these conflicts. Vietnam withdrew from Cambodia in 1989, and a peace agreement was signed in 1991.

Painful memories

Over the years, the Vietnamese have tried to repair the damage to their country. Buildings, roads, bridges, railroads, and factories have gradually been rebuilt. Some Americans returned to Vietnam to help rebuild. Most Vietnamese lost friends and family members who were killed or fled the country. Many who survived the war were badly injured. In spite of so many setbacks, the people of Vietnam work hard to make their country a stable and prosperous nation.

(top) Thousands of Vietnamese lost their homes during the war. They were forced to live in refugee camps that were set up across the country.

(below) American soldiers fought with the South Vietnamese army against communist forces.

Cities

Although most Vietnamese live on farms, in the past several years many have moved to large cities and towns located in the lowlands or on the coast. Hanoi and Ho Chi Minh City are large, modern, crowded centers, whereas other cities, such as Hué and Dalat, are smaller and quieter.

Hanoi

Hanoi is located in Northern Vietnam in the Red River Delta. It is Vietnam's capital and is the center of government for a united Vietnam. Built on the banks of the Red River, its name means "city at the bend of the river." With a population of three and a half million, it is Vietnam's second-largest city and an important industrial center in the north.

Hanoi's business section, hotels, and shops are in an area that was built by the French in colonial times. The wide streets are lined with trees, and the buildings have iron balconies and painted shutters. The city is famous for its many lakes and beautiful parks. In the heart of its downtown area is Hoan Kiem Lake, or the Lake of the Restored Sword. It is surrounded by a large park where families and friends have picnics, fly kites, celebrate festivals, or just go for a stroll. Along the park, people can be seen practicing *tai chi* in the mornings.

Hanoi's long history can be seen in its ancient temples and **pagodas**, built during Chinese rule. Vietnam's first university was built in Hanoi in 1076 during the Ly Dynasty.

(above) Bustling Ho Chi Minh City has become a center of international business. The city has more businesses and industry than any other city in Vietnam.

Ho Chi Minh City

Ho Chi Minh City and its surrounding farmland is home to almost five million people and covers a large area of 783 square miles (2,029 square kilometers) in the Mekong Delta. The streets are filled with bicycles, motorcycles, cars and buses, and the sidewalks are crowded with people selling goods. The traffic is noisy and music blaring from cafés and apartments fills the air.

A mix of sights and sounds

Like Hanoi, Ho Chi Minh City has French colonial architecture and culture. You can still buy croissants and French baguettes in the markets. Many of the wide streets in the downtown area are lined with trees and tall skyscrapers. Until 1976, this city was called Saigon. When it was taken over by the North Vietnamese army, it was renamed Ho Chi Minh City, after the leader Ho Chi Minh, who led the rebellion against French control. Local people still refer to the downtown core of the city as Saigon. Close to the downtown core is the bustling Chinese neighborhood known as Cholon, which means "big market."

Hué

Hué is a quiet city in central Vietnam with a population of 286,400 people. Hué was the capital city of the Nguyen Dynasty, which lasted from 1802 to 1945. Thirteen emperors ruled during that time. A walled fort, called the Citadel, surrounds much of the city. Inside is the Forbidden Purple City where the emperors lived. Most of the Forbidden Purple City was destroyed during the Vietnam War. Many people have worked to restore its beauty.

Dalat

Dalat is a small city located in the Central Highlands. It was founded in 1987 by the French. Dalat is often called the "City of Eternal Spring" because the weather is mild and sunny for most of the year. It is one of the most scenic and beautiful cities in Vietnam. There are many parks, forests, lakes, waterfalls, and flower gardens in and around the city. Dalat is a popular vacation spot, especially for Vietnamese couples on their honeymoon. Several thousand hill tribe peoples make their home in Dalat.

(above) This archway in Hué is the gate to Emperor Tu Duc's tomb. Tu Duc reigned from 1848 to 1883.

(left) Hué is Vietnam's third-largest city and is an important cultural, educational, and religious center.

17

(above) Vietnamese farmers grow a wide variety of crops, such as potatoes, corn, tomatoes, beans, peas, sweet potatoes, cabbage, and tropical fruit, which are sold at village and city markets.

Farming

Today, fifteen percent of Vietnam's land is used for farming. About 70 percent of the people are farmers. Farming in Vietnam is difficult work. Most farmers do not have tractors or other modern equipment. They use water buffalo to help with heavy work such as plowing or carrying crops. Other jobs, such as planting and harvesting, must be done by hand.

Rice—a vital crop

Rice has been farmed in Vietnam for thousands of years. Today, three-quarters of the country's farmland is used for growing this crop. Most rice farms are located in the river deltas. The deltas are perfect for growing rice because of their rich soil, warm weather, and plentiful water supply. Farmers can grow two or three crops each year. Farmers now grow more rice than the Vietnamese need, so the extra rice is exported, or sold to other countries. Vietnam is the world's second-largest exporter of rice, after Thailand.

Other crops

Cash crops are farmed mainly to sell to other countries and are grown on large plantations. In the mist-covered hills of the highland regions, tea and coffee are harvested. In the south,

rubber trees are tapped for their valuable sap, used in making rubber. Sugar cane, pepper, and peanuts are other valuable cash crops.

Fruits and vegetables

Many fruits and vegetables grow in Vietnam's moist, warm climate. Bananas, pineapples, mangoes, and coconuts are sold in the local markets. Sweet potatoes, tomatoes, snow peas, cabbage, and cassava, a shrub whose roots are eaten, are popular vegetable crops.

Terraced farmlands

Farmers in the northern and central highlands use terraces to grow crops on steep hills. Terraces look like giant steps. When heavy rains fall on hills, fertile soil is washed down into valleys and streams. This process is called soil erosion. Terraces stop soil erosion because they are flat. The rainwater is held on the steps and soaks into the ground. In some countries, farmers have grown crops on terraces for thousands of years.

(below) Modern farms use bulldozers and other machines to build terraces. In Vietnam, the terraces were cut into the hills by hand!

 # Growing rice

Rice is grown in fields called paddies. Farmers grow it in either dry or flooded paddies. Others use a combination of dry and wet paddies. They scatter seeds in the dry paddy, water them, and wait for them to sprout into tiny plants, or seedlings, before moving them to a wet paddy.

Preparing the fields

It takes about one month for the seedlings to grow. During this time, the farmers busily prepare their wet fields for the little plants. They build low dikes around the paddies. All day long, entire families collect water in straw baskets and carry it back to flood the paddy. When the seedlings are tall enough, they are carefully pulled from the dry paddy, tied into bundles, and carried to the flooded paddy. One by one, the seedlings are planted in neat rows in the mud. Even while the plants are growing, the farmers do not rest. They are busy weeding and flooding their fields. As the plants grow, the water level in the paddy is raised. Soon the small rice plants grow tall and green, and all the hard work is rewarded.

Harvest time

When the rice plants turn a golden color, they are ready to be harvested. Farmers open the dikes to drain the water from the paddies. The rice plants are cut by hand, using a sharp, curved knife. They are then bundled and laid out in the sun to dry.

Threshing

Threshing, which separates the rice grains from the stalk of the plant, is usually done by beating the plants against bamboo poles. Farmers who live near a highway often spread their rice right onto the road. The hot, flat surface not only dries the grains faster, but passing cars and trucks drive over the rice and help with the threshing.

(above) A farmer prepares his paddy. Farmers in the delta regions grow rice in wet paddies, but farmers in the northern regions grow a variety of rice using only dry paddies.

(opposite page, top) Workers place bundles of rice plants in the wet mud of the paddy.

Milling and winnowing

When the rice is dry, it is gathered into baskets and pounded. This process, called milling, separates the rice kernel from its brown husk. In the final step, called winnowing, basketfuls of milled rice are tossed into the air so the wind can blow the light husks away from the kernels.

Nothing is wasted

Vietnamese farmers use every part of the rice plant. The husks are fed to farm animals, and the stalks are woven into mats or used as fertilizer. After the family takes what it needs for food, the rice kernels are gathered into sacks. Then they are shipped off to city markets or sold to other countries.

(above) Winnowing is often done by hand using large, flat baskets.

Harvest from the sea

Vietnam's long stretch of coastline lends itself to the fishing communities in villages and cities along the sea. Each morning, the coastal villages of Vietnam come alive with activity as fishing boats prepare to set out to sea. Some boats are small and use oars, but most are sailboats or motorboats. Anchovies, mackerel, cuttlefish, snapper and lobster are hauled out of the sea in large nets. Men and women wait on the beach to help pull in the heavy catch. Prawns, crabs, and shrimp are caught in the inland waterways.

Fish farming

Farming fish is a popular business in villages close to waterways. The fish are kept in pens to keep them from escaping. The pens are created by enclosing parts of a river or stream. Farmers feed their fish special food to make them grow big and fat. Carp, catfish, and long river-dwelling fish called snakehead are among the fish raised in these farms. Shrimp are farmed in the canals of the Mekong River Delta.

An important food source

Seafood is an important part of the Vietnamese diet. Millions of people depend on the fishing industry for their daily meals. A salty fish sauce made from anchovies is a common cooking ingredient. Mixed with garlic, vinegar, and sugar, this sauce becomes *nuoc cham*, a tasty dip for many foods.

Fish for profit

Many people also rely on fishing for their income. Fish caught off the coast are sold to other countries, especially Japan. Some Vietnamese sell their catch at fish markets, where people buy fresh seafood for their families or for restaurant customers.

(above) Mieu Island, near Nha Trang, along the central coast, is one of the most important fish farming areas in Vietnam. The cuttlefish held by this fish farmer is not actually a fish; it is a close relative of the octopus and squid.

(left) These frozen fish are emptied from the hold of the larger blue boat after a week of deep-sea fishing off the coast of Nha Trang. The smaller boats take the fish to the shore.

(opposite page, top) Reeling in the heavy nets used to catch fish in the surrounding sea is a big job.

(opposite page, bottom) When smaller fishing boats come into harbor, the catch is often pulled ashore in large baskets. Carrying these heavy loads takes teamwork!

Transportation

Traveling long distances in Vietnam is not always easy. Roads and highways are often washed out by floods and monsoon rains. Few people can afford cars. Trains are slow, and flying is expensive. Most people who have to travel long distances take the bus or train.

On the water

There are so many rivers and canals that one of the easiest ways to travel is on the water. Every day, thousands of boats transport people and goods from place to place. Small flat-bottomed boats, called sampans, travel rivers and streams. Long, narrow boats carry larger loads. Traditional sailboats, called **junks**, cruise along the coast.

Two wheels or three?

City streets are crowded with thousands of bicycles and motorcycles. In the north, bicycles are the main means of transportation for millions of people. In the south, more people own motorcycles. The traditional Vietnamese taxi is the *Xe Lam*, a small three-wheeled vehicle. Another easy way of getting around the city is by *xich-lo*, or cyclo, a three-wheeled bicycle. It has a passenger seat in the front and one for the driver in the back.

(top) Round boats called thung chai *are made of woven bamboo strips covered with tar.*

(above) Bicycles of all kinds are an inexpensive means of travel for Vietnamese families.

(right) A Xe Lam is a popular way to get from place to place in a big city.

Road rules

Traveling on Vietnam's roads can be a risky undertaking. Drivers speed through towns and cities as they weave between other vehicles, pedestrians, and bicycles. Trucks, cars, and buses blare their horns at every turn. Vietnam's major highway, called Highway One, stretches from the Chinese border in the north to Ho Chi Minh City in the south. In rural areas, farmers spread their rice and wares along the roadway like a market.

Animal power

On the rough dirt roads of villages, animals are still an important means of transportation. Most farmers cannot afford a car or truck. Instead, they use water buffalo to pull carts.

The *Reunification Express*

When Vietnam was a French colony, its rulers built a railroad to connect Hanoi and Saigon (now Ho Chi Minh City). During the Vietnam War, the rail lines were damaged by bombing. After the country was united, the Vietnamese government began rebuilding the railroad to link the north and the south. It takes one and a half to two days for the slow-moving *Reunification Express* to make the journey between Hanoi and Ho Chi Minh City.

(above) Buffalo boys are young workers who look after water buffalo.

(below) Passengers get ready to board a train at a station in Lang Son in northeastern Vietnam.

New business

A country's economy is the organization and management of its businesses, industry, and money. After years of terrible warfare, Vietnam faced the difficult task of rebuilding its economy. The communist government took control of the land, banks, and factories.

Hard times

When the communist government took over the south in 1976, many business people fled the country. When Vietnamese soldiers invaded Cambodia in 1978, many foreign countries boycotted, or refused to trade **raw materials** or **manufactured goods** with Vietnam. The communist government built factories and set up large farms. People were expected to work for the government and could not own a business or land. Workers were poorly paid and Vietnam's economy suffered. Harvests were low and millions of people were unemployed.

New ideas

In 1986, the government **reformed** its economy by introducing a policy called *doi moi*, which means "new thinking." Some farmers were allowed to rent land, and small family businesses began to appear all over the country.

Trading with the world

In 1989, when the Vietnamese government pulled its soldiers from Cambodia, other countries lifted their boycott of the country. As part of *doi moi*, the government allowed foreign companies and banks to set up offices in Vietnam. Countries that had refused to trade with Vietnam now rushed to invest their money in Vietnamese businesses. Small business of all kinds prospered.

(below) In the 1990s, many foreign companies set up businesses in Vietnam.

All kinds of products

The ability to trade with more countries around the world sparked a revival of Vietnam's economy. Shops, restaurants, and hotels opened across the country. Small factories began to manufacture bicycles, glass, bricks, and other products. Artisans created beautiful **textiles** and **ceramics** that could be sold. Street markets filled with once-scarce fruits and vegetables.

One step back

The economic growth from *doi moi* lasted only a few years. By the mid-1990s, many of Vietnam's natural resources had been used up. Thousands of people moved from rural areas to work in the cities. The unemployment rate increased and there was an increase in crime in the cities. Vietnam is still learning to operate under its new economic reforms. Although the government now allows foreign and private business to operate, as a communist country it still wants to control all business affairs. There are many restrictions and rules which discourage businesses and investors from other countries.

New hope

Vietnam is trying to improve its economy and create business with other countries. Currently Vietnam's biggest trading partners are Japan and Singapore. The country's biggest exported goods are coal, petroleum, peanuts, rice, rubber, tea, and bamboo products. In 2000, Vietnam signed a trade agreement with the United States. The Vietnamese people are especially fond of North American products. American-made computers, pagers, and soft drinks are popular. Chain restaurants, such as Kentucky Fried Chicken and Baskin Robbins, have also been welcomed to the country.

(above) Two brothers stand proudly behind the counter of their family-run shop. Since the mid-1980s, Vietnamese people have had the freedom to own their own businesses.

Plants and wildlife

Vietnam has a variety of wild animal **habitats** because it has so many different regions and climates. These habitats are home to over 270 species of mammals, 800 species of birds, and hundreds of species of reptiles, fish, and amphibians. In addition, new animals are being discovered in Vietnam's remote forests. A rare species of deer, several types of frogs, and a large relative of the cow called the Vu Quang Ox have been recently identified by scientists.

In the wild

Animals commonly seen in Vietnam are cattle, water buffalo, monkeys, dogs, cats, pigs, goats, ducks, chickens, and squirrels. **Tapirs**, tigers, leopards, bears, deer, otters, and porcupines are some of the wild animals that live in Vietnam's forests. Sea birds nest in the deltas along the coast, and fish and amphibians thrive in the coral reefs and warm coastal waters.

Reptiles

There are over 180 species of reptiles in Vietnam. These include snakes such as pythons and cobras, and many types of lizards, such as geckoes, monitor lizards, agamid lizards, and flying lizards. Crocodiles, tortoises, and turtles live in the **mangrove** swamps of the south.

Plant life

Vietnam's forests are home to more than 12,000 plant species. In the north, there are rhododendron and bamboo forests. Some areas of rainforest remain in the mountain regions. Pine and evergreen forests appear in the central areas of the country. Valuable hardwoods such as ebony and teak grow in the central and southern regions. Mangrove forests grow in the river delta areas. Many types of tropical fruit trees, such as banana, mango, orange, papaya, and coconut, grow in southern Vietnam.

(left) Sea turtles are illegally hunted, and their shells are used to decorate combs, jewelry, and boxes.

Endangered species

Many forested areas in Vietnam were destroyed by the war, and continue to be cut down by loggers and farmers. When forests disappear, animals cannot find food or homes, so they also disappear. Many of the animals that live in Vietnam's wilderness are **endangered**, and some species, such as the Sumatran rhinoceros, are already **extinct**. Endangered species include the Javan rhinoceros, the Asian elephant, the golden-headed langur, and the douc langur.

Protection

To protect endangered animal habitats and to prevent further deforestation, the government has set aside land for several national parks. In all, there are ten national parks and several reserves. The government is planning to set aside more land for parks. Unfortunately, there is not enough money to hire the park staff needed to prevent poachers from hunting the endangered animals. The illegal hunting and selling of endangered animals continues. The government has also started a reforestation program in an attempt to rebuild Vietnam's forests.

(opposite page) The douc langur, a rare mammal, is easily recognized by the red-tipped fur on its cheeks.

(right) More than 600 bird species can be found in southern Vietnam alone.

(above) Some Asian elephants are kept as work animals. Very few survive in Vietnam's wilderness.

A changing Vietnam

There have been many improvements in Vietnam in recent years. People are earning more money and are able to buy more of the things they need. Along with these improvements, however, there are also new challenges.

Changing values

Now that many countries are able to do business in Vietnam, the country is being introduced to more foreign customs and products. Tourists and business people from Europe and North America visit Vietnam each year and introduce their ways of life to the Vietnamese. These new ways are especially attractive to young people. As a result, attitudes are changing along with fashions, music, and lifestyles. Some people are afraid that their lives will change so much that their old values will be lost. Others believe that change is a necessary part of progress.

Population boom

Vietnam's population has grown rapidly in the last twenty years. The population is expected to double in the next one hundred years. Overpopulation presents a challenge for the government. It is difficult to provide resources such as food, housing, jobs, and health care to a larger population. Vietnam's government is trying to reduce population growth by encouraging people to have only one or two children. Parents who have one or two children are promised extra benefits, such as better jobs, education, and health care.

(below) One third of Vietnam's population is under the age of fifteen. Vietnamese people have traditionally had large families, but the government is now encouraging parents to have fewer children.

Poverty

Over the past decade the unemployment rate in Vietnam's cities has risen. Factories owned by other countries have shut down and more people have moved to the cities hoping to find work, only to find none. To make ends meet, many people create their own income by selling goods, exchanging money for foreign travelers, or crime. Millions of people, including children, are homeless and living on the streets.

Pollution

The main cause of pollution is Vietnam's industries. Offices and factories need electricity to make products and operate computers. To get enough electricity, more energy plants are built. Unfortunately, many of these plants burn coal to make electricity. Coal creates a black smoke that makes the air very dirty. Motorcycles also add to the pollution problem. As well, more tourists now visit Vietnam, so resorts are being built along the South China Sea. The water is being polluted, and beaches, coral reefs, and mangrove swamps have been destroyed.

Wasting land

Vietnam's valuable forests are disappearing rapidly. Only one quarter of its ancient forests are left. During the war, sixteen percent of forested land in South Vietnam was destroyed by bombing and Agent Orange. The forests that were lost could have supplied timber for Vietnam for thirty years. Today, loggers cut down trees to sell as lumber to other countries. In other areas, farmers are cutting down forests so they can plant more crops. When the crops deplete the soil of its nutrients, the farmers cut down more forested area. Trees are also being cut down to be used as firewood for heating and cooking in many homes.

(above) Some residents of Ho Chi Minh City live in poverty beside the dirty Mekong River. Garbage and industrial waste have polluted the water.

(right) The logging industry is contributing to the destruction of Vietnam's forests. Government projects to plant new trees have not yet replaced the vast number of trees that have been cut down.

Glossary

altitude The height of the earth's surface above sea level

cash crop A crop grown mainly for export

ceramic Pottery that has been glazed and baked at very high temperatures

Christianity A religion based on the teachings of Jesus Christ, who is believed to be the son of God

communism An economic system in which the country's natural resources, businesses, farms, and industry are owned by the government

corrupt Dishonest

doi moi A term describing Vietnam's new economic ideas and changes

endangered Describing a plant or animal species that could soon become extinct

equator An imaginary line that runs around the center of the earth

extinct No longer in existence

habitat The natural environment in which a plant or animal lives

junk A large flat-bottomed sailboat with square sails and a square front

mangrove A type of tropical tree that grows in wet areas such as swamps

manufactured goods Any items that are made in factories using machines

monsoon A system of seasonal winds and rains in Southern Asia

natural resources Materials found in nature, such as oil, coal, minerals, and lumber, which are useful to humans

pagoda A temple that is usually tower-shaped and found in eastern countries

plantation A large farm on which only one crop is grown

raw material A substance from the earth that is not yet processed or refined

reform To change something in order to make corrections or improvements

refugee A person who leaves his or her home or country because of danger

tai chi A martial art involving a series of body movements, used as exercise and to balance one's energy

tapir A short, long-snouted rhinoceros-like animal

terrace A piece of earth, usually on a hill, with a flat top that is used for growing crops

textile Any type of woven or knitted fabric

Viet Cong South Vietnamese who supported the communist government during the Vietnam War

 # Index

1 2 3 4 5 6 7 8 9 0 Printed in the USA 0 9 8 7 6 5 4 3 2 1